TOWER HAMLETS

KU-183-119

91 000 006 200 58 8

SCARED SILLY
Jokes & Riddles

MICHAEL J. PELLOWSKI

STERLING CHILDREN'S BOOKS
New York

To Butch, Bandit, Spud,
Little Spike, and Spooky Cat

STERLING CHILDREN'S BOOKS
New York

An Imprint of Sterling Publishing Co., Inc.
1166 Avenue of the Americas
New York, NY 10036

STERLING CHILDREN'S BOOKS and the distinctive Sterling Children's Books logo
are registered trademarks of Sterling Publishing Co., Inc.

© 2017 by Sterling Children's Books

All rights reserved. No part of this publication may be reproduced, stored
in a retrieval system, or transmitted in any form or by any means (including
electronic, mechanical, photocopying, recording, or otherwise) without prior
written permission from the publisher.

ISBN 978-1-4549-2256-8

Distributed in Canada by Sterling Publishing Co., Inc.
c/o Canadian Manda Group, 664 Annette Street
Toronto, Ontario, Canada M6S 2C8
Distributed in the United Kingdom by GMC Distribution Services
Castle Place, 166 High Street, Lewes, East Sussex, England BN7 1XU
Distributed in Australia by NewSouth Books
45 Beach Street, Coogee, NSW 2034, Australia

For information about custom editions, special sales, and premium and
corporate purchases, please contact Sterling Special Sales at 800-805-5489 or
specialsales@sterlingpublishing.com.

Manufactured in Canada

Lot #:
2 4 6 8 10 9 7 5 3 1
03/17

www.sterlingpublishing.com

Design by Ryan Thomann

Contents

HA HA HA HA HA HA

1

FULL MOON MADNESS

What do you call a bunch of werewolves who tell fibs?

A pack of liars.

Who did the skeleton nominee bring to the political convention?

All of the delegates it could dig up.

Knock-knock!

Who's there?

Antilles.

Antilles who?

Antilles in his coffin, we're not safe from Count Dracula.

SIGN IN A ZOMBIE ELEMENTARY SCHOOL
Walk, Don't Run!

MEL: Why are you so frightened?
NELL: I heard that zombies eat brains.
MEL: Relax. With a brain like yours, you have nothing to be afraid of.

Why don't vampires attack zombies?
   Because zombies have stiff necks.

Knock-knock!
   Who's there?
Ivanna.
   Ivanna who?
Ivanna bite your neck!

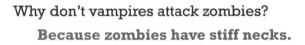

BOO!

NIGHT NOTICE
Vampires are light sleepers.

Why did the vampire die after attacking Chewbacca?

It choked on a hair ball.

What did the hipster call the Wolf Man who was a total loser?

A going no-werewolf.

How does the top werewolf send a letter?

He uses alpha-mail.

How do you keep a sick zombie active?

Put it on a non-life-support system.

── STARS OF THE NEW ──
WEREWOLF MOVIE

Hairy Fellows

Hugh Beast

Kay Niner

Luna Bright

I. Emma Howler

Why are zombies always so tired?
Because they never return to their last resting place.

Then there was the dumb salesman who tried to sell suntan lotion to vampires.

Why did the specter sailors drown when their vessel sank?
Because their ship didn't have a lifeboat.

Show me a ghost who never makes the right decision . . . and I'll show you a creature who's always dead wrong.

What do you call a very tired wolf man?
A weary wolf.

Who is the most depressed zombie?
The one who won a five-thousand-dollars-a-week-for-life lottery prize.

What did the musician ghouls name their band?
The Rocking Undead.

Knock-knock!
> Who's there?

Allen.
> Allen who?

Allen favor of tracking down the sea monster, say aye!

Show me a swamp creature who loves his job … and I'll show you a creature who drowns himself in his work.

Where can you find the Wolf Man on social media?
> **Look on Hairy-Facebook.**

What do you get if you cross an audio track with Count Dracula?
> **Sound bites.**

SKYLER: Did you know that there are zombie astronauts?
TYLER: Yes. Let's go and blast them off the planet.

LUKE: Did you hear about the zombie professor who attacked his best student?
DUKE: I sure did! Now he's the dead head of the class.

MONSTER FAVORITES

Favorite pop song: "Not Living La Vida Loca"

Favorite action movie: *Die Hard*

Favorite play: *Death of a Salesman*

Favorite western song: "Bury Me Not
on the Lone Prairie"

Favorite spy movie: *Don't Live and Let Live*

Favorite soap opera: *No Life to Live*

Why did the vampire go to the witch doctor?
He had a bat case of the flu.

How did Dracula catch a cold?
**He forgot to close his coffin
on a chilly winter's day.**

Why was the zombie banker
so sad?
**He lost his
life savings.**

What did the skeleton
put on his mashed potatoes?
Grave-y.

HORROR STORY TITLE

Hunting Monsters at Night by Cary A. Torch

NIGHT NOTICE

The vampire dog's bite is worse than his bark.

Knock-knock!
> **Who's there?**

Thad.
> **Thad who?**

Thad guy is a mad scientist! Let's get out of here!

MATT: Do zombies write with ink pens?

PAT: No. They use grave markers.

What do you call a group of young, rude werewolves?
> **A brat pack.**

How can you tell if a werewolf is very hungry?
> **Its stomach will howl really loud.**

Why can't zombies become extinct?
> **Because they never die out.**

Some people see death as the big sleep. Zombies see it as a short nap before taking a walk.

Who is Zombie Moby Dick?

He's the wailing undead.

NICK: Did you hear about the electrician who died?
RICK: No—this is shocking news. When did it happen?
NICK: Just after fate pulled the plug on him.
RICK: What a shame. He used to be such a live wire.

CREEPY QUESTION

Do the deceased laugh at deadpan humor?

Knock-knock.

Who's there?

I, Lloyd.

I, Lloyd who?

I Lloyd when I said I wasn't a witch.

KNOCK-KNOCK!

What does an author do after he becomes a ghost?

He pens his last writes.

What do you call a baby vampire?

A night crawler.

— INVENTIONS TRANSYLVANIANS NEED —

Bite-proof turtleneck sweaters

Shirts with cast-iron collars

Wolfsbane-scented deodorant

Cement-topped graves

Full moon sirens

Garlic-scented perfume

JUDY: I once saw a vampire turn into a bat.

RUDY: That's nothing—I once saw a zombie who turned into a pizza restaurant.

What did the timekeeper use to destroy Count Dracula?

A minute stake.

NIGHTLY NEWS FLASH!

Mummy actors refuse to work in front of a live audience.

What did the zombie say when a voodoo witch doctor jumped out of the shadows?

"You scared the life out of me!"

Why did the vampire lose his job?

He couldn't work the day shift.

What games do gangster mad scientists play?

Corpse-and-grave robbers.

What did Mummy Nathan Hale say before he was hanged by the redcoats?

"I regret that I have no life to give for my country."

How did Godzilla get to be president of the monsters' union?

He smashed the competition.

Why didn't the teenage girl go to the skeleton hair stylist?

She didn't want to dye too young.

What do you get if you cross Count Dracula with Sir Lancelot?

A bite in shining armor.

Knock-knock!

Who's there?

Hugh Sheen.

Hugh Sheen who?

Hugh Sheen any evil clowns around here?

What did the zombie say to the band leader?

"I want to sing a capella, so kill the music."

ZOMBIE EMCEE: Is that a live Mike on stage?

STAGEHAND: No, it's that undead comic—
Rob D. Grave.

What is a zombie's favorite tree?

A mul-bury tree.

IGOR: I have to take a mummy exam.

IVAN: Are you worried about it?

IGOR: Yes. I'm scared to death of failing.

Why don't ghosts ever duel?

Because they can't fight to the death—
they're already dead!

How do you capture a ghoul?

Use an after-death trap.

What kind of people do zombies hate the most?

A part of people do zombies hate the most?

What kind of people do zombies hate the most?

Pet owners who don't clean up after their dogs.

What do you call a corpse that wins the lottery?

A lucky stiff.

Knock-knock!

Who's there?

Dee.

Dee who?

Dee-stroy all monsters!

DARK DAFFYNITION

Funeral parlor: an eternal rest home

Why don't normal people live in skyscrapers?

Because they're full of horror stories.

Knock-knock!

Who's there?

I, Betty.

I, Betty who?

I Betty turns into a werewolf when the full
moon rises.

What do you call the legal title to a property owned by a zombie?

The walking deed.

Knock-knock!

Who's there?

Luke.

Luke who?

Luke out! Here comes the creature from the Black Lagoon!

HEADLINE ON A
POLTERGEIST OUTLAW POSTER
WANTED: UNDEAD OR NOT ALIVE.

What do you get if you cross a werewolf with King Kong?

A really big howler monkey.

What do you call a zombie who has two broken legs?

A night crawler.

2

FANGS VERY MUCH

What happens after an angry vampire lies down in his coffin?

He flips his lid.

DARK DAFFYNITION

Count Dracula: the original bat-man

Why did Count Dracula move to Las Vegas?

He was a big fan of the nightlife.

HA HA HA

How can you tell if a zombie is also a vampire?

If he's a vampire, he'll drac his feet when he walks.

What is Detective Godzilla's main objective as a police officer?

He wants to take a big bite out of crime.

FRIGHT FACT

Since a lot of vampires are from Transylvania, maybe it would be more appropriate to spell the name of their homeland "Transyl-vein-ia"!

ODD VAMPIRE OCCUPATIONS AND MOTTOS

Poultry farmer Dracula: "Don't count your chickens before they hatch."

Prizefighter Dracula: "Never count me out."

Math teacher Dracula: "You can count on me."

Astronaut Dracula: "You can now start the Count-down."

How does a poltergeist get a driver's license?

It takes its death certificate to the DMV (Dead Motor Vehicles) Agency.

What kind of ship does Captain Dracula sail?

A blood vessel.

Why is it impossible to shock a skeleton?

Because a skeleton doesn't have a spark of life left in it.

What do you call a wolf man who wears jeans and a polo shirt to work?

A casual-wear–wolf.

DARK DAFFYNITION

Corn specter: a night stalker

When does a driver's license become an apparition?

After it expires.

What do male zombies put on their faces in the morning?

After-grave lotion.

FRIGHT FACT

Mr. Werewolf is King Kong's mane man.

Why did the zombie jump into the river?
   It heard that fish are brain food.

What is one job a vampire can never have?
   A vampire can never be a day laborer.

DARK DAFFYNITION

Zombees: a horror buzz word

What is Attila the Hun's ghost called?
   He's the leader of the Hun-dead.

Then there was the vampire with a bad back who slept in a Craftmatic® coffin.

Where does Dracula have tea and crumpets?
   At the Count-Tea Morgue.

CREEPY QUESTIONS

When does a football player become a zombie?
After he kicks off.

When does a real-estate agent become a zombie?
After she buys the farm.

When does a casino gambler become a zombie?
After he cashes in his chips.

When does a hotel guest become a zombie?
After she checks out for the last time.

When does an actor become a zombie?
After the final curtain falls.

When does a watchmaker become a zombie?
After his time runs out.

When does a cowboy become a zombie?
After his last roundup.

When does a math teacher become a zombie?
After her number is up.

SIGN ON A VAMPIRE HOSPITAL
Blood Donors Wanted.

Knock-knock!
> Who's there?

Ice cream.
> Ice cream who?

Ice cream when I see goblins.

What did Count Dracula call his moving work of art?
> A bat-mobile.

Why did the werewolf football player move to Green Bay, Wisconsin?
> He wanted to be a wolf Packer.

Knock-knock!
> Who's there?

Theodore.
> Theodore who?

Theodore to the haunted house is wide open.

How do you destroy a provolone vampire?
> Drive a cheese-stake through its heart.

Why did Mr. and Mrs. Zombie get a divorce?

Because they vowed to stay wedded only "until death do us part."

Knock-knock!

Who's there?

Gwen.

Gwen who?

Gwen you see an evil witch, run away quick.

Why don't werewolves and vampires attack track runners?

They don't like fast food.

Does a zombie ostrich bury its head in the sand?

Yes, but not for long.

MONSTER MOTTO

Vampire mulch company:
"Our bark is not worse than our bite!"

How do corpse soldiers go from place to place?

A funeral march.

What is Batman's ghost?

The Dark Knight of the living dead.

Why did the vampire become an author?

It had a lot of write blood cells.

Knock-knock!

Who's there?

Bea.

Bea who?

Someone from Bea-yond the grave.

HA HA HA HA HA HA HA HA HA

Do vampire bats stay at motels when they travel?

No. They stay at cave inns.

What kind of creatures do you find in Atlantic City?

The boardwalking dead.

Why don't vampires attack skeletons?

Because there's nothing for them to sink their teeth into.

What is one thing ghosts never have to worry about?

The high cost of living.

How do you imprison a vampire?
    Put it in a red blood cell.

Knock-knock!
    Who's there?
Less Al.
    Less Al who?
Less Al track Count Dracula
to his resting place.

What do you call a zombie
who cheats on her boyfriend?
    The unfaithful undead.

Knock! Knock!
    Who's there?
Howie.
    Howie who?
Howie escaped from that Yeti I'll never know.

SIGN OUTSIDE A GRAVEYARD
Warning! Dead Ahead!

IVAN: What did you think of the new vampire play on Broadway?

IGOR: I loved it. The leading actors sucked the life out of their roles.

IVAN: Do you think a zombie would make a meal of my brain?

IGOR: No. Your brain is so small, it would only be a snack.

What specter was a Confederate general during the Civil War?

   General Dead Lee.

Why didn't the zombies go on the Ark before the Great Flood?

   Because there were Noah brains on board.

3

What did the Walking Dead track team nickname the zombie who ran the 100-yard dash in under three hours?
    Speedy.

Knock-knock!
    Who's there?
Rob Bing.
    Rob Bing who?
Rob Bing graves is a horrible crime.

HA HA HA HA HA

What kind of ghost wears spurs?

One that was originally buried in Boot Hill.

What happens when you scare a timid ghoul?

It faints dead away.

Why do nice people become poltergeists?

Because all good things must come to a dead end.

How can you tell if a zombie is a fitness freak?

If it's a fitness freak, it'll be a speed-walking dead.

What is a dark spirit?

One that's had the living daylights scared out of it.

Why did the robot become a ghost-bot?

Because it just could not rust in peace.

Why won't zombies go to the beach?

Because they're afraid someone will bury them in the sand.

What did the host of Corpse Jeopardy say at the end of the show?

"**Hearse your final answer!**"

Why did the zombie go to the beach?

It wanted to dead-bodysurf.

DARK DAFFYNITION

Zombieland: a wonderful place to not live

Zombieville: a bury nice town

GHOST MILLIE: When my boyfriend broke up with me I said, "I'll never get over it as long as I live."
GHOST TILLIE: And what happened?
GHOST MILLIE: Well, I'm over it now.

How does a surfer zombie track down its victims?

It follows their brain waves.

Knock-knock!

Who's there?

Hugo.

Hugo who?

Hugo for help before the goblins get here!

What is Dr. Frankenstein's favorite place to vacation?

The Dead Sea.

Why did Grandpa Zombie buy a motorized wheelchair?

He was tired of walking dead.

NIGHTLY NEWS FLASH!

Then there was the Norse zombie who had Thor feet.

What do you call very old zombies?

The walker undead.

DARK DAFFYNITION

Body language: a conversation between mummies

FRIGHT FLASH!

To become a witch pilot, you have to graduate from fright school.

HORACE: Did you hear about the really clumsy zombie?

BORIS: No. Which one is he?

HORACE: He's the walking dead with two left feet.

Why did the giant spider and giant squid go to the mall?

Because the mall was having a monstrous sale.

SIGN IN AN UNDERWORLD LIBRARY
Dead silence at all times!

IVAN: Do you like my paintings?

IGOR: Yes. They're monsterpieces.

What kind of a bike does a zombie ride?

A no-life cycle.

Why did the corpse declare bankruptcy?

He was buried in debt.

IVAN: Did you hear about the ghost convict?

IGOR: No.

IVAN: He was a former lifer.

When do zombies wake up for the first time?
First thing in the moaning.

Why didn't the flashlight work?
It had dead batteries.

Where does a ghoul keep its valuables?
In a cemetery vault.

What does an undead sailor wear if his ship sinks?
An afterlife jacket.

Knock-knock!
Who's there?
I, Ester.
I, Ester who?
I Ester to stay away from haunted houses,
but she didn't listen to me.

IVAN: Did you hear
about the outbreak of
undead farmers?
IGOR: No.
IVAN: They're cropping
up everywhere.

4

DARK HUMOR

Where is the best place to re-bury a corpse?
In a fiendish plot.

Knock-knock!
   Who's there?
Deers.
   Deers who?
Deers another
evil clown over
there!

HORROR STORY TITLE

Everything You Want to Know About Monsters
by Vera Curie Yuss

Knock-knock!
  Who's there?
Ray.
  Ray who?
No—who-ray! The evil sorcerer is defeated!

When did the daredevil become a dead-devil?
  After he failed to make a death-defying leap.

What is the most famous Greek zombie ruin?
  The Zombie Acropolis.

And then there was the vampire
umpire who was blind as a bat.

What do you get when you
cross a vampire with a
mortgage officer?
  A blood banker.

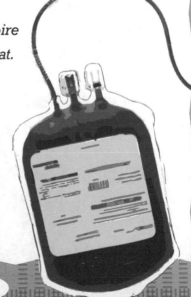

What do you get when you cross a hickory tree with a wolf man?

A nutty timber wolf.

What creepy athletic event takes weeks to complete?

The Walking Dead Marathon.

DARK DAFFYNITION

Dead heat: a skeleton with a fever

Why is Zombie Town such a dull place?

It has absolutely no nightlife.

Why didn't the werewolf go out when the moon was full?

He was just too dog-tired.

What's the worst thing you can get from a yeti?

Frostbite.

Knock-knock!

Who's there?

Irish.

Irish who?

Irish those goblins would go away and leave us alone.

Why don't vampires ever get into fistfights?

They're afraid someone will knock their teeth out.

KNOCK-KNOCK!

MONSTER MOTTO

Happy zombies: "Every day is bury nice."

What do you call a hobo's ghost?

A deadbeat.

What did the monster say when it entered the all-night deli?

"I just dropped by for a quick bite."

JOE: I heard you just bought a new grave plot.
MOE: That's right. I got it dirt cheap.

DARK DAFFYNITION

Skeleton super soldier: a tombsday weapon

Then there was the lonely vampire who loved in vein.

BORIS: Did you hear the story about the evil horses?

HORACE: Yes. It's a whoa-ful tale.

What kind of lamps do werewolves have in their homes?

    Moon lights.

CREEPY QUESTIONS

Can a hungry ghost starve to death?

Do werewolves get fleas?

What happens when a mosquito bites a vampire?

Do vampire bats need rabies shots?

Do old werewolves ever go bald?

Do old vampires use fang dentures?

What happens if an astronaut werewolf lands
on the moon?

Knock-knock!

Who's there?

A. Churchill.

A. Churchill who?

A. Churchill be a safe place to hide from vampires!

Which zombie is a famous baseball player?

Bury Bonds.

What is a vampire's least favorite day of the week?

Sunday.

What do you get if you cross a corny comedian with a corpse?

The pun-dead.

What is a young witch doctor's favorite toy?

A voodoo doll.

What does a flock of geese get when it sees a mob of monsters?

Severe goose bumps.

What is a werewolf's favorite day of the week?

Moonday.

FRIGHT FLASH!

Evil butchers are dying to meat you.

Where do cowboy mummies come from?
Tombstone, Arizona.

Knock-knock!
Who's there?
Water.
Water who?
Water you—an evil
witch or an evil warlock?

IVANNA: Vampires can't see their faces in mirrors.
IGOR: Does that go for lady vampires, too?
IVANNA: Yes.
IGOR: Then how do they put on makeup?

ARMY CAPTAIN: Hey, soldier! Stop leaning
against that post and look alive!
ZOMBIE PRIVATE: Sorry, sir. No can do.

*Then there was the ghost who was afraid of going out
in the cold—he didn't want to catch his death.*

Why did the mummy workers go on strike?

They wanted a higher un-living wage.

Why did the skeleton go to the police station?

He was held up by a grave robber.

Knock-knock!

Who's there?

Dewey.

Dewey who?

Dewey have a good place to hide from swamp monsters?

IGOR: What does a person have to do to become a zombie?

IVAN: Oh, just drop dead.

Why did the judge order the prisoner to be released?

His conviction was a grave miscarriage of justice.

What happens when a vampire and a werewolf have an argument?

They fight tooth and nail.

Knock-knock!
  Who's there?
Caesar.
  Caesar who?
Caesar! She's an evil witch trying to escape!

Where in the Pacific were the Zombie Marines stationed?
  On Wake Island.

How did Count Dracula disappear from sight?
  He used a cloaking device.

How did the ghoul bar his front door?
  He used a dead bolt.

What's the best light to turn on when a vampire breaks into your house?
  A sunlamp.

What do you put in the tank of a werewolf's car?
  The fuel moon.

5

Knock-knock!

Who's there?

Otto.

Otto who?

Otto my way! An evil clown is coming!

Knock! Knock!

Who's there?

Karl.

Karl who?

Karl up with a good book and
stay inside at night to keep safe.

BOO!

Why do Land of Oz monsters like to attack Munchkins?

Because they're bite-size.

Which cowboy are werewolves most afraid of?

The Lone Ranger. He has lots of silver bullets.

IGOR: Why did that werewolf run away when he saw us?

IVAN: I guess he was wearing a flee collar.

What do you get when you cross a wolf man and an ewe?

A werewolf in sheep's clothing.

Knock-knock!

Who's there?

Hy Shaw.

Hy Shaw who?

Hy Shaw a monster hiding in the lake.

What do you get when you cross one kilogram of water with a wolf man?

The liter of the pack.

Which werewolf goes on a lot of hikes?

The wolf cub scout master.

Why did the banshee shriek at the television?

It was a widescream TV.

WOLF MAN: Help me, Doc. I'm sick as a dog.
VET: Really? Your nose doesn't feel warm or dry.

Why does snobby Mrs. Werewolf like it when the full moon rises?

It gives her a chance to show off her fur coat.

SPIKE: I'm the greatest wolf man in history.
IKE: Hmph! That's just a doggie brag.

GODZILLA: I think I should bite your head off!
VICTIM: Now that's a snap decision.

BORIS: Who does a sick werewolf go to for treatment? A doctor or a vet?

NORRIS: It depends.

BORIS: On what?

NORRIS: If the moon is full or not.

DRACULA: Will the ghost agree to join our monsters' union?

WOLF MAN: No. He's dead set against joining.

Why are werewolves so hotheaded in June, July, and August?

Because they have to wear a fur coat in the summer.

MACK: I think that vampire is flirting with me.

ZACK: What makes you say that?

MACK: She keeps batting her eyelashes at me.

Why do skeletons fear werewolves?

Because all canines like to bury bones.

What do you get when you cross Wolf Man with Batman?

A hairy crime fighter that chases Catwoman up a tree.

DETECTIVE: I just arrested the Wolf Man.
POLICE CHIEF: Bravo! That's a big dog collar.

What is an oak wolf man?

It's a werewolf that barks instead of howls.

Knock-knock!

Who's there?

Werewolves.

Werewolves who?

Werewolves are, you won't find me.

KNOCK-KNOCK!

Show me a fancy formal dance for werewolves . . . and I'll show you a Fur Ball.

Why was the zombie wolf man so happy?

He had a new leash on life.

How can you tell if a werewolf is a snob?

A snobby werewolf prowls around with its nose up in the air.

What do you get when you cross a werewolf with a French dog?

A werepoodle.

What do you call a she-wolf who wears high-fashion clothing?

A designer werewolf.

LITTLE GHOUL: My father was a wolf man when he passed away.
BIG GHOUL: Now that's a doggone shame.

Knock-knock!

Who's there?

Howell.

Howell who?

Howell we escape if an evil warlock attacks us?

Knock-knock!

Who's there?

Police.

Police who?

Police open the door! The aliens are after me!

6

Why did the zombie drown?
**Because the other zombies
wouldn't throw it a lifeline.**

What does a mummy get if it talks
too much in its grave?
A dirty mouth.

HA HA HA HA HA
HA HA HA
HA HA
HA HA

ZOMBIE #1: I'm going to hunt rabbits for our dinner.

ZOMBIE #2: Now that's a hare-brained scheme.

Why don't zombies go out in thunderstorms?

They're afraid they'll get hit by a dead bolt of lightning.

Who was Count van Gogh?

He was the first artist to draw blood.

— STARS OF —
HORROR MOVIES

Barry Me

Ewell Scream

Dee Ceased

M.T. Graves

Henrietta Brain

Indy Morgue

Which zombie was a member of King Arthur's Round Table?

The Knight of the Living Dead.

What country makes designer jeans for vampires?

Pantsylvania.

Why did the ghost call 9-1-1?

It was faced with a no-life or death decision.

POLTERGEIST ARTIST: Do you like my
self-portrait?
CRITIC: I do. It's so un-lifelike.

Which fantasy creature do vampires fear the most?

The Tooth Fairy.

GIANT SQUID: Why are you shaking all over?
SPIRIT: Sea monsters scare the life out of me.
GIANT SQUID: Don't be a dope! You're already dead.

Why was the ghost so sad?

His life's work proved to
be only temporary
employment.

How did the convicts' spirits
escape prison?

It was easy. Prison has
no lifeguards.

Why did the corpse go to a chiropractor?

He had stiff joints.

What did the ordinary ghost say to the celebrity specter?

"I've been dying to meet you."

What courses are offered at universities in the afterlife?

Everything except life sciences.

BOY ZOMBIE #1: That zombie girl always seems so put together.
BOY ZOMBIE #2: I agree. She has a cool no-lifestyle.

What has fangs, feathers, and quacks?

Count Duckula.

How do you write a great novel?

Start with a grave plot.

What's the difference between a giant lollipop and a vampire?

One is an all-day sucker and the other is an all-night sucker.

FRIGHT FLASH!

When the full moon rises, fun-loving werewolves go to their neighborhood preyground.

Why was the deceased gambler so angry?
He never got a second chance at life.

What's the dumbest thing you can say to an annoying zombie?
Take a hike, dude!

What do zombies get when they eat ice cream that is too cold?
A brain freeze.

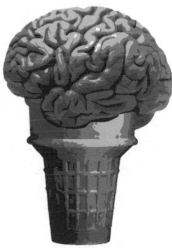

What is a vampire's favorite Italian city?
Veinice.

Dungeon: where creepy crawlies like to hang out

Why did the Poltergeist Punks cancel their world tour?

They could no longer perform live.

ZOMBIE #1: I just heard that the voodoo witch doctor plans to stick me in a grave.
ZOMBIE #2: That sounds like a burial plot to me.

What is a vampire's favorite flavor of ice cream?

Veinilla.

NIGHT NOTICE

A corpse with a steady job is a working stiff.

What is a vampire's favorite racket sport?

Batminton.

Knock-knock!

Who's there?

Les Barrymore.

Les Barrymore who?

Les Barrymore werewolves so the world will be a safer place.

What do you call a zombie duck?

A waddling dead.

Knock-knock!

Who's there?

Ivan.

Ivan who?

Ivan running away from mad scientists all night.

Why did Count Dracula join the circus?

He wanted to be an acrobat.

How did the newlywed ghosts spend their honeymoon?

They went for a cruise on the Dead Sea.

What does Count Dracula wear while riding his motorcycle?

A batting helmet.

Knock-knock!
> Who's there?

Ken Hugh.
> Ken Hugh who?

Ken Hugh please not bite my neck?

What do you call newlywed werewolves?
> **Honey-full-mooners.**

What do you use when you arrive at a zombie's front door?
> **A dead ringer.**

Then there was the zombie sailor who was buried at sea and ended up in a sub plot.

What do you get if you cross a vampire with a sobbing werewolf?
> **A bat and bawl.**

Why did the umpire call the vampire out at the plate?
> **The vampire batted out of turn.**

What vampire whines all the time?

   Pout Dracula.

Why did the mad scientist yearn for the brain
of Einstein?

   His doctor told him to study smart.

Knock-knock!

   Who's there?

Whale.

   Whale who?

Whale be going to the cemetery to hunt
for grave robbers.

HA HA HA HA
HA HA HA HA
HA HA HA HA
HA HA

7

BITING HUMOR

Why did Dracula bite the old prospector?
He was hoping to find a vein of gold.

ATTENTION!

The fishing is great in Transylvania because
vampire fish are always biting!

Knock-knock!
> Who's there?

Frank Lee.
> Frank Lee who?

Frank Lee, I don't believe in ghosts.

What is a 50-percent zombie?
> One that's half dead.

KNOCK-KNOCK!

MONSTER MOTTO

Vampires' Italian restaurant: "We don't use garlic in any of our recipes."

Why did the skeleton cattle ranch go broke?
> It had no livestock.

Why don't monsters like refereed wrestling matches?
> Because no biting is allowed.

Knock-knock!
> Who's there?

Asia.
> Asia who?

Asia house mummy-proof?

Why did the goblin flunk out of vampire school?

He failed his blood test.

Where can you find zombie kittens in Rome, Italy?

Look in the cat-acombs.

Why did the zombies attack the fitness center?

They wanted to eat something healthy.

What did the spirit say to the funny comedian?

"If I wasn't already dead, your jokes would kill me."

MONSTER MOTTO

Werewolf police: "No matter where you run, you can't escape the long arm of the claw!"

ZOMBIE #1: I'm starving! I want food! Now what do you think about that?

ZOMBIE #2: Calm down and I'll give you a piece of my mind.

Knock-knock!

Who's there?

Titus.

Titus who?

Titus mummy to a tree and use plenty of rope.

What is a 25-percent werewolf?

One that transforms during the quarter moon.

What kind of victim does a dieting vampire
prey upon?

One with low blood sugar.

*Then there was the undead competitive eater who'd
lived a full life.*

What do you get when you cross a monster
with a bull?

A creature to steer clear of.

HORROR HOW-TO

How do you destroy a rabid milk cow?
   Cream-ate it!

How do you destroy a demonic cabbage?
   Chop off its head!

How do you destroy an ivy villain?
   Poison ivy!

How do you destroy a destructive potato?
   Mash it!

How do you destroy a flesh-eating fly?
   Call in a swat team!

How do you destroy an evil balloon?
   Stick a pin in it!

How do you destroy deathly crabgrass?
   Mow it down!

How do you destroy poisonous dust?
   Blow it away!

Knock-knock!

Who's there?

Harold.

Harold who?

Harold is King Kong? I'll bet he's at least one hundred.

What do you call a vampire who has severe psychological problems?

A basket-casket case.

BORIS: Did you hear the rumor about the zombie hairdresser?

HORACE: Yes, but that story doesn't set well with me.

Where did the spirit of Seabiscuit finish in the race?

First. After all, you can't beat a dead horse.

Knock-knock!

Who's there?

Oscar.

Oscar who?

Oscar what she's dressing up as for Halloween.

Which vampire eats too much junk food?

Count Snackula.

Why do English corpses never smile?

Because they always keep a stiff upper lip.

What has fangs, claws, fur, and hibernates during the winter?

A werebearwolf.

Where do you take a dented zombie to be repaired?

To an undead body shop.

Then there was the Hollywood monster who became a movie star by playing bit parts.

Then there was the other Hollywood monster who was dying for a role he could really sink his teeth into.

What did Judge Vampire say to his coffin at daybreak?

"I think it's time to close this case."

DESERT RAT: How did you obtain the vampire's silver mine?

PROSPECTOR: I staked a claim on it.

How do you keep a corpse's sandwich fresh?

Put it in a body baggie.

Knock-knock!

Who's there?

Dairy.

Dairy who?

Dairy is! It's the Creature from the Black Lagoon!

How did the cowboy get a filthy mouth?

It bit the dust.

DARK DAFFYNITION

Zombie: a down-to-earth monster

How do you catch a fisherman ghoul?

Use live bait.

Where does a vampire wash her hands?

In the batroom sink.

Why did the skeleton have a lump on his noggin?

When he got up, he bumped his headstone.

Who is the hippest vampire?

Count Dracoola.

What do you get when you cross a zombie with a gopher?

A zombie that doesn't unearth itself; it just tunnels around instead.

Why won't a vampire from the Land of Oz bite the Tin Man?

Because the Tin Man has too much iron in his blood.

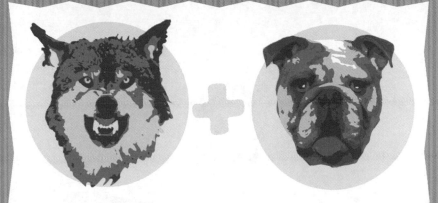

What do you get when you cross a werewolf with a bulldog?

A wolf man with a stubby tail.

How can you tell if a vampire is a fussy eater?

If it's a fussy eater it won't bite your neck . . . it'll just peck at it.

What is a ghost's favorite candy?

After-life savers.

What do you get when you cross a zombie with bread dough?

A zombie who rises when the sun bakes on its grave.

Then there was the hippie corpse who was laid to rest in a bed of flowers.

8

SHADOW SNICKERS

What do you call a zombie couch potato?
An undead too lazy to walk.

Why don't zombies attack stupid people?
The answer to that is a no-brainer.

How did the police detective catch the criminal vampire?

He staked out his coffin.

How does a werewolf track down a vampire?

It follows the scent of blood.

VAMPIRE: Help! Help me quick! The top of my coffin is missing.

WOLF MAN: Oh, quit yelling and put a lid on it already.

THE SCREAM FAMILY

Hy Scream

Hugh Scream

Wee Al Scream

Flora I. Scream

What do you call ghosts who rise up in the morning?

The waking dead.

Then there was the spoiled corpse who would only sleep on rich soil.

Where do vampire ducks swim?
In a pool of blood.

───────── CREEPY QUESTION ─────────
Are stupid zombies brain-dead?
─────────────────────────────────

What did the monster use to fix his broken fang?
Toothpaste.

Then there was the night crawler who wormed his way out of the grave.

GOBLIN: Stop all that loud howling before you wake the dead.
WEREWOLF: Oh, mind your own business! They're already up and walking around.

Why doesn't anyone listen to the ghosts' radio station?

Because it broadcasts nothing but dead air.

FRIGHT FACT

Zombies are life-after-death creatures who become death-after-life creatures.

How does a dirty monster get clean?

It takes a bloodbath.

Show me an embarrassed vampire . . . and I'll show you a night stalker who is a bloody shame.

How do you destroy a sirloin-crazed vampire?

Take it to a stake house.

MONSTER MOTTO

Vampire fox: "Once bitten, twice sly."

What do you get when you cross a wolf man with a sled dog?

A werewolf with a brain full of "Mush!"

Where do rabid minnows swim?

In a bloodstream.

What did the victim say to the undead sailor?

"Take a long walk down a short pier."

What do you get when you cross a flock of geese with zombies?

A brain-hungry mob that heads south for the winter.

What is the most dangerous job in Transylvania?

Being a vampire dentist.

Why is Dracula in charge of all vampires?

He's the Head Count.

DRAC: How was the werewolf convention?

WOLFIE: It was a howling success.

MUMMY #1: Do you know where you left your crypt keys?

MUMMY #2: No. And I can't remember for the life of me.

Knock-knock!

Who's there?

I, Ben.

I, Ben who?

I Ben haunted by a poltergeist.

How did the police collect criminal evidence against Count Dracula?

They went on a stakeout.

9

GET-A-LIFE LAUGHS

What happens if you use ghoul shampoo?

Your hair ends up with lifeless body.

Who was in charge of the corpses' movie?

The funeral director.

What is Dracula's favorite rhyme?

A tisket, a tasket, a dirt-filled vampire's casket!

Knock-knock!

Who's there?

X.

X who?

X-plain how you became a witch doctor.

IVAN: I just saw a bloodthirsty dairy cow.

IGOR: That's udderly impossible.

Knock-knock!

Who's there?

V.

V who?

V better run for our lives!

Knock-knock!

Who's there?

U. B.

U. B. who?

U. B. careful if you go out tonight.

Knock-knock!

Who's there?

Y. R. U.

Y. R. U. who?

Y. R. U. trying to bite me?

Knock-knock!

Who's there?

Q.

Q who?

Q me if you see a monster backstage.

Knock-knock!

Who's there?

I. Z.

I. Z. who?

I. Z. you hiding behind that tombstone.

Why was the debutante's corpse so depressed?

Because she led a luxurious life
and now she's dirt poor.

What do you get when a vampire
hog gets caught out in the sun?

Crisp bacon.

Why was the spirit so upset?

It thought its existence was
a living nightmare.

Knock-knock!

Who's there?

I, Zena.

I, Zena who?

I Zena banshee and a witch.

What did the corpse say to his employer before he was cremated?

"Please, boss, don't fire me!"

ZOEY: What's the best way to attract zombies?

JOEY: I can't think of anything.

ZOEY: Well, use your brain.

What funny time travel flick did Michael J. Vampire star in?

Bat to the Future.

Why are ghosts and ghouls so carefree?

They're never faced with life or death decisions.

What advice did the grownup monster give to the munchkin monster?

"Take small bites."

What do you put on a zombie lamp?

A deadly nightshade.

Knock-knock!

Who's there?

It's Usher.

It's Usher who?

It's Usher them. Destroy
the monsters!

*Then there was the tidy corpse who always lined
her grave with clean dirt.*

BARRY: Ghosts do exist!

HARRY: Humph! There's no living proof of that.

What kind of deals do salesmen give their customers
on household appliances in the underworld?

No lifetime guarantees.

Knock-knock!

Who's there?

Dear Lee Dee.

Dear Lee Dee who?

Dear Lee Dee-parted.

Why was Little Dracula punished?
Because he'd been a bat boy.

What makes up a class of dead people?
Student bodies.

When did the tired mailman become a zombie?
After he lost all of his zip.

SINISTER SIGN ON A FUNERAL HOME
Pay, or Rest Without Peace

What does a fairy godmother's evil spirit do?
She grants death wishes.

Why did the vampire bite a ghost?
It wanted to try a victim that had boo blood in its veins.

DARK DAFFYNITION

Monster computer chips: life bytes

Knock-knock!
>Who's there?

Earl Lee Dee.
>Earl Lee Dee who?

Earl Lee Dee-mise.

KNOCK-KNOCK!

MRS. CANNIBAL: New people just moved into the house next door.

MR. CANNIBAL: Great! Let's have them over for dinner tonight.

How do you put out the candles on an evil spirit's birthday cake?
>Use a deadly blow.

Knock-knock!
>Who's there?

Eerie.
>Eerie who?

Eerie go again, chasing zombies.

Then there was the mattress salesman who became a poltergeist for the unrest of his life.

WITCH DOCTOR: Now take a deep breath.

PATIENT: Okay, but it'll be my last gasp.

ROBBER: Your money, or your life.

MUMMY: Ha! I'll just keep my money, pal!

BEN: I've been a jogger all of my life.

JEN: Face the facts—your life has run its course.

AFTERLIFE ROLL CALL

Noah Pulse

Cole Body

Barry D. Bunch

Etta Lotta Brains

Morg Slab

Dee Kayed

Why did the spectators flee from the basketball star?

He was known to be a deadly shot.

HA HA HA HA HA HA

What's the best way to study zombies?

Examine a non-living specimen.

Why was the football tackle worried about becoming a ghost?

He realized that the end was near.

Knock-knock!

Who's there?

Weaver.

Weaver who?

Weaver alone, you horrible creature!

DARK DAFFYNITION

Underworld bucks and does:

the deerly departed

IVAN: What's that?

IGOR: It's a ghost time clock.

IVAN: How does it work?

IGOR: When people come to work as ghosts, they punch out for good.

IVAN: I've been told that there are no dead in that boarding house.

MONSTER HUNTER: Hmph! I think that's just a living roomer.

Knock-knock!
> Who's there?

Les Hyde.
> Les Hyde who?

Les Hyde quick! Here comes an evil warlock.

GHASTLY GUS: I have hundreds of skeletons under me at my new job.

GHOULY GERTIE: What do you do?

GHASTLY GUS: I'm the night watchman at the graveyard.

What holiday do ghosts in Wonderland always celebrate?

Their undead unbirthdays.

What kind of corpse walks around with dumbbells?

The undead body builder.

Knock-knock!

Who's there?

I, Helda.

I, Helda who?

I Helda vampire at bay with a handful of garlic.

What do you get when you cross a werewolf with a grizzly?

A very furry wolf man that eventually goes bear.

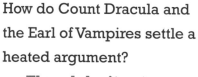

How do Count Dracula and the Earl of Vampires settle a heated argument?

They duke it out.

Then there was the romantic member of the walking dead who took a nightly stroll down memory lane.

What do you get if you cross a bloodthirsty mosquito with an evil praying mantis?

A biting insect that is a holy terror.

Knock-knock!
Who's there?
Hearse.
Hearse who?
Hearse to you, Mr. Mummy. Drink up!

Knock-knock!
Who's there?
Sahara.
Sahara who?
Sahara we going to destroy that sea monster?

What do you get when you cross Count Dracula with a minister?
A vampire that says a Hail Mary before biting your neck.

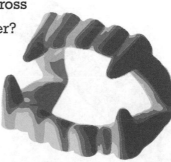

What do you get when you cross a zombie duck with a zombie rooster?

The quack of dawn.

How did the exorcist get rich?

He scared the devil out of a lot of customers.

Knock-knock!

Who's there?

Wendy.

Wendy who?

Wendy witching hour starts, ghouls and ghosts come out to play.

What do you get when you cross Dracula with a brontosaurus?

A vampire that sleeps in the biggest coffin you've ever seen.

BOO!

Did you hear about the witch doctor's doll? It operates on dead batteries.

Knock-knock!

    Who's there?

Stan.

    Stan who?

Stan back! I'm going into that haunted house!

10

DRAC'S LAUGH ATTACK

Knock-knock!

Who's there?

Amos.

Amos who?

Amos find a safe place to hide.

KNOCK-KNOCK!

DARK DAFFYNITION

Holy demon: an evil spirit who spends a
lot of time trying to prey

Knock-knock!

> Who's there?

Kenny.

> Kenny who?

Kenny summon a spirit whenever he wants to?

Why do the undead look so stiff when they walk?

> **Their underwear is too tight.**

What's the most dangerous job during the full moon?

> **Being an animal control officer.**

Knock-knock!

> Who's there?

Voodoo.

> Voodoo who?

Voodoo you think it is?

What happened to the vampire toast when the sun popped up?

It burned to a crisp.

Knock-knock!

Who's there?

Saber.

Saber who?

Saber from that beast—it's about to attack!

MONSTER MOTTO

Transylvanian medical alert: "A clove of garlic a day keeps the vampires at bay!"

Knock-knock!

Who's there?

Witch.

Witch who?

Witch is more scary, a swamp creature or a giant spider?

HA HA HA HA HA HA HA HA HA

Afterlife's Amtrak: a fright train

Why did Count Dracula walk around in his pajamas?

Because he didn't own a batrobe.

What's a good way to make friends with a werewolf?

Give him a box of doggie treats.

What screams and rolls down the street during the witching hour?

A banshee wearing Rollerblades.

What do you call a very old werewolf?

A greyhound.

Knock-knock!

Who's there?

Al Bloch.

Al Bloch who?

Al Bloch the door. You bar the window.

What do you get when you cross stray cats with the undead?

Zombies that hunger for mouse and bird brains.

Why did Count Dracula go to the blood bank?

He heard they were looking for volunteers.

Knock-knock!

Who's there?

Arthur.

Arthur who?

Arthur any creepy crawlies in this spooky old forest?

What does a vampire stand on while it takes a shower?
A no-slip batmat.

What has one wheel and gets twenty-five miles to a gallon of plasma?
A vampire on a unicycle.

SINISTER SIGN IN A MUSIC STUDIO

Don't let classical music die!
Bring Johann Sebastian Bach to life.

What happens if a hearse gets caught speeding?
It has to pay a stiff fine.

Why is a zombie baseball game boring to watch?
Because the batters always walk.

Why do vampires have unhealthy diets?
They enjoy too many midnight snacks.

HA HA HA HA HA HA HA HA HA HA HA HA HA

Knock-knock!

Who's there?

Ewe.

Ewe who?

Ewe scared the wits out of me!

Why was the broke werewolf chasing his tail?

He was trying to make ends meet.

Then there was the famous movie producer who only made underworld films.

What do zombies get if they go barefoot in the snow?

Walking pneumonia.

Why doesn't Dracula eat a lot of expensive desserts?

They're too rich for his blood.

Why didn't the shy corpse go out at night?

He was a homebody.

Knock-knock!

Who's there?

Weevil.

Weevil who?

Weevil heard enough scary jokes for one day.